One
Day
This
Tree
Will
Fall

# One Day This Tree Will Fall

Leslie Barnard Booth

Illustrated by Stephanie Fizer Coleman

MARGARET K. McELDERRY BOOKS
New York  London  Toronto  Sydney  New Delhi

MARGARET K. McELDERRY BOOKS
An imprint of Simon & Schuster
Children's Publishing Division
1230 Avenue of the Americas,
New York, New York 10020

MARGARET K. McELDERRY BOOKS is a
trademark of Simon & Schuster, Inc.
Simon & Schuster: Celebrating 100 Years
of Publishing in 2024
For information about special discounts
for bulk purchases, please contact
Simon & Schuster Special Sales
at 1-866-506-1949 or
business@simonandschuster.com.
The Simon & Schuster Speakers Bureau
can bring authors to your live event. For
more information or to book an event, contact
the Simon & Schuster Speakers Bureau
at 1-866-248-3049 or visit our website at
www.simonspeakers.com.
The text for this book was set in Avenir.
This book was painted using gouache,
colored pencil, and Photoshop.
Manufactured in China
1123 SCP
First Edition
2 4 6 8 10 9 7 5 3 1
Library of Congress
Cataloging-in-Publication Data
Names: Barnard Booth, Leslie, author. |
Coleman, Stephanie Fizer, illustrator. Title:
One day this tree will fall / Leslie Barnard
Booth ; illustrated by Stephanie Fizer
Coleman. Description: First edition. |
New York : Margaret K. McElderry Books,
2024. | Includes bibliographical references. |
Audience: Grades 2-3. | Summary: A tree's
life story is told from its beginnings as a
seed to its survival in the wilderness until it
finally falls, but continues its life as a log, an
animal habitat, and finally decomposes to
provide nutrition for future trees. Identifiers:
LCCN 2023010237 | ISBN 9781534496965
(hardcover) | ISBN 9781534496972 (ebook)
Subjects: CYAC: Trees—Fiction. | Forests
and forestry—Fiction. | Life cycles—Fiction. |
LCGFT: Picture books. Classification: LCC
PZ7.1.B37095 On 2024 | DDC [E]—dc23
LC record available at
https://lccn.loc.gov/2023010237

For Iris and Azalea, now and always
—L. B. B.

For Seth, always
—S. F. C.

LOOK AT IT.

Wounded, worn, twisted, torn.
One day this tree will fall
and this story will end.

Won't it?

First, you should know
that long, long ago . . .

a tiny seed set sail.
Folded inside it
was a tiny tree—
*this tree.*

Other seeds flew too.
Some landed on bare rock. Or drowned
in a stream.
Most were simply
gobbled
up.

This tree's story might have ended that day.

But it didn't.

This tree grew.

And grew . . .

despite wind

despite ice

despite
   drought
      drought
         drought.

Then,
a spark.

Something crackled to life in the dark.
Something wild.

Something ravenous.
Something made entirely of flame.

This tree's story might have ended that day.

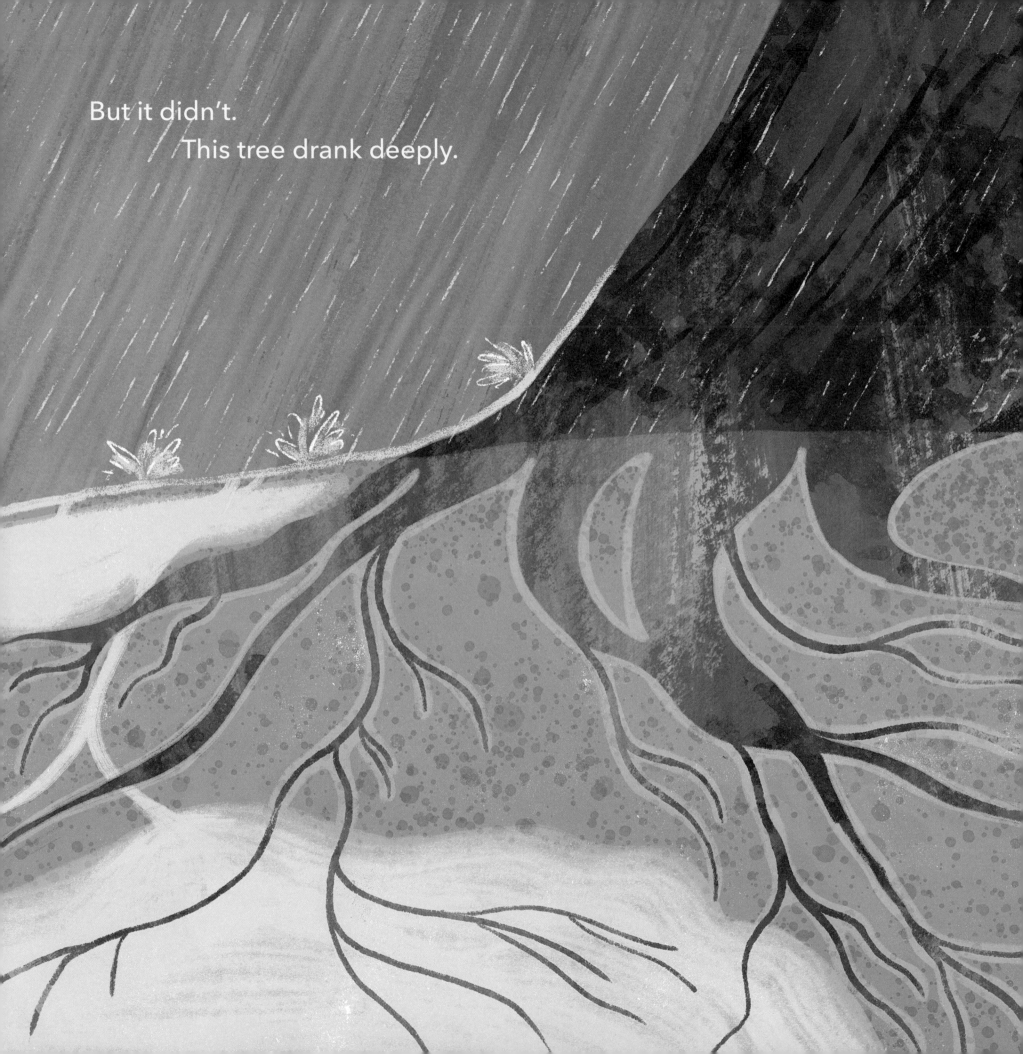

But it didn't.
This tree drank deeply.

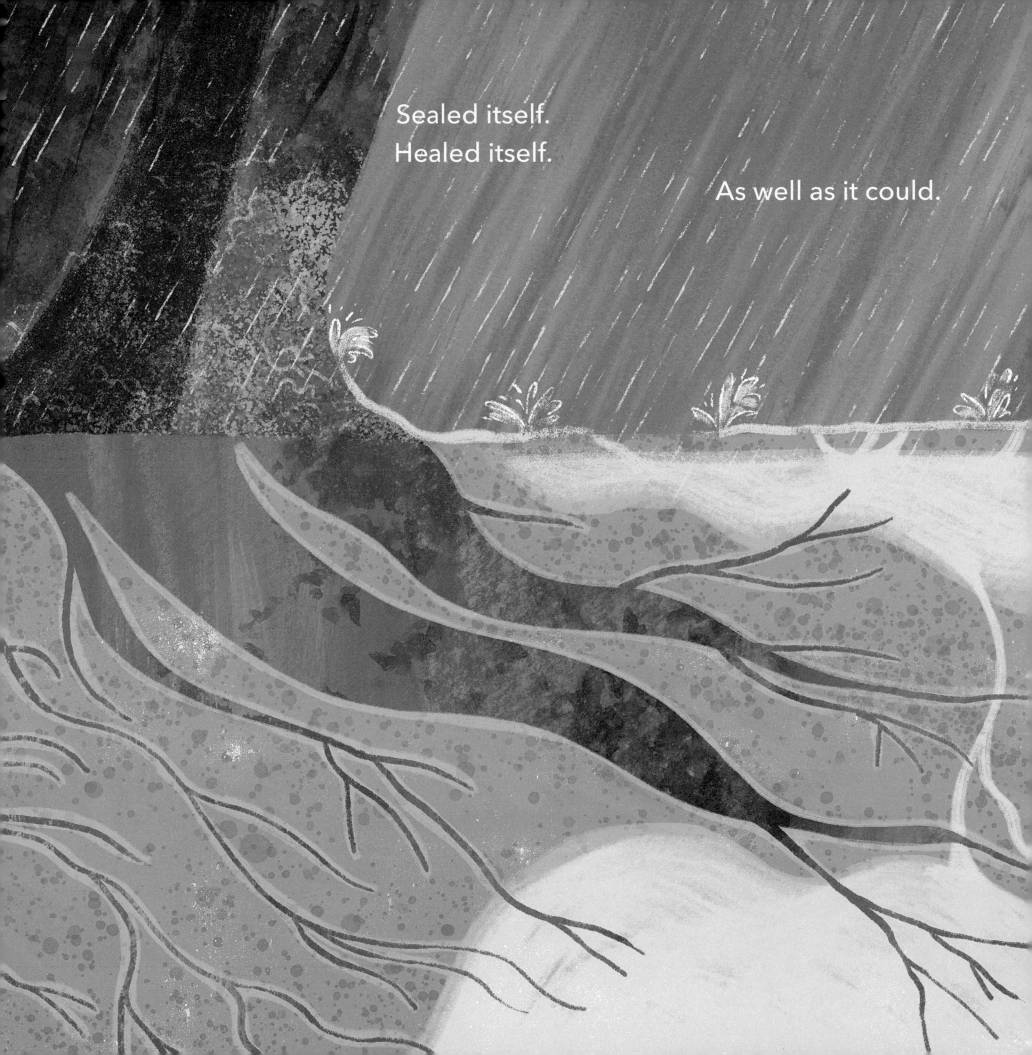

Sealed itself.
Healed itself.

As well as it could.

Meanwhile,
the creatures of the forest
nibbled

clipped

clawed.

And humans . . .
humans hauled giants away.
But
not
this
one.

This tree . . .

*Survived.*
This tree touched the sky.
By now, it was so much more than a plant.
   It was a place.
It was a *world*
of miniature forests
meadows
rivers
seas,
of silken death traps
and venomous fangs,
   of bright, begging mouths
      and fluttering wings.

This tree flourished.

This tree aged.

Some of its wounds never closed.
Some opened.
    Some grew.
    But no crack or crevice ever went to waste
    because this tree
continued to be
a roost
    a nest
        a den.

                Then—

its last trace
of green growth
faded.

This tree's story might have ended that day.

But it didn't.
And it won't.
*Ever.*

*Yes, yes—one day this tree will fall . . .*

that rocks the forest.

But even when this tree is just a log . . .

it will *still* be a place
where moss gathers and mushrooms bloom,
where rain erodes and mold consumes,

where a secret city brims
   with workers, soldiers, queens,
where salamanders guard their eggs
   and cougars crouch unseen . . .

where winter casts a sleeping spell,

then releases it in spring . . .

where snakes slither
and slime spreads,
    where earwigs and earthworms

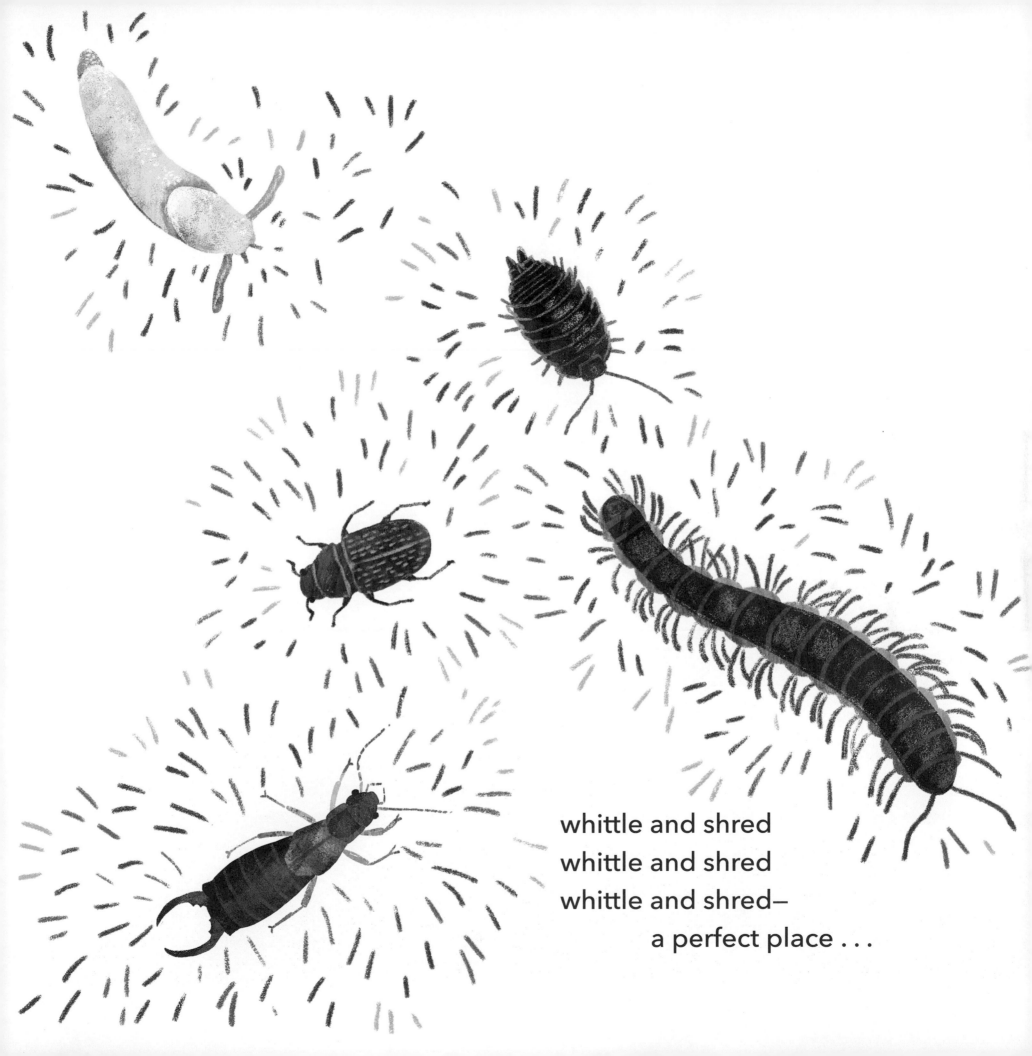

whittle and shred
whittle and shred
whittle and shred—
a perfect place . . .

for the next seed to settle

. and sprout

and grow.

# A Tree's Story Never Ends

Most people recognize young, healthy trees as an essential part of any forest. But trees that are damaged, dying, or dead are critical to the functioning of the forest ecosystem too. As they slowly decay, these durable structures provide nourishment and habitat for thousands of species—including the next generation of trees.

## LIFE

Trees are among Earth's most long-lived organisms. Douglas firs, like the one in this book, can live for over 1,000 years.

When a tree is young, its structure tends to be simple and uniform. Its stem is straight. Its bark is smooth and bare. It doesn't house much wildlife yet. As time passes, though, a tree's structure changes. Patches of moss and lichen accumulate on its increasingly rough and wrinkled bark. Its shape becomes distinctive as its limbs strain toward sunlight or bend against wind. Over the years, it also suffers from injury and disease, acquiring holes, scars, and dead or broken limbs.

All of these imperfections make an aging tree's structure more complex. This allows it to house a larger number and wider variety of organisms. Insects inhabit every region of its varied landscape—from its sunlit canopy to its rain-filled holes. Amphibians slip into its fissures, and birds and rodents find well-concealed nesting sites among its tangled branches.

Damage leads to more damage—and to expanded opportunities for wildlife. Any openings in the tree's protective bark serve as portals for rot and disease. Wounds also attract invertebrates such as beetles and ants, which bore into the tree and lay eggs. Woodpeckers follow, probing the tree to get at the larvae inside.

A woodpecker may also use its chisel-like bill to excavate a nesting hole in a weakened tree. This nesting cavity remains after the woodpecker's chicks are grown, and it becomes a valuable resource for diverse wildlife, including songbirds, ducks, owls, and small mammals. Because these creatures need cavities to raise their young, their survival depends on woodpeckers—and on damaged or dead trees.

## DEATH

Snags, or standing dead trees, are important habitat structures. Raptors perch on snags to scan for prey. Bats, butterflies, and frogs shelter under their peeling bark. Many other forest animals nest, rest, or den in their holes and hollow chambers.

When a snag topples, it instantly delivers a huge, elaborate, nutrient-packed structure to the forest floor. Some of the snag's inhabitants are forced to flee, but other creatures flourish. Beetles, termites, and other wood-feeding invertebrates thrive, and their network of tunnels expands. They are accompanied by decomposers (mostly fungi and bacteria), which spread throughout the log, consuming it further. Insect eaters, such as spiders, centipedes, and snakes, join the community too.

The log doesn't just provide food—it also protects wildlife from the elements. Amphibians wriggle under it to stay moist and hidden. Rodents spend winter curled inside it. Hollow chambers shelter large mammals, including bobcats, foxes, and wolves. Bears seek out the largest hollows, where they hibernate and give birth to their cubs.

But that's not all . . .

## LIFE AFTER DEATH

Through a process called photosynthesis, trees use the sun's energy to make food out of water and air. Trees use this food—along with additional nutrients mined from the soil—to build their physical structures. A dead tree still contains these ingredients, which happen to be precisely the same substances new plants need in order to grow.

But living plants can't just suck these substances out of dead wood. The wood must first be broken down into a form plants can use. This process is called decomposition, and it is exactly what's happening as all of those invertebrates and decomposers feed on the log. Invertebrates jump-start the decomposition process as they chew, chop, and shred. Fungi and bacteria digest dead matter even further, unlocking the vital nutrients inside it and releasing them back into the environment.

Slowly but surely, these organisms accomplish something astounding. They convert a massive, sturdy structure into a soft, moist, crumbly mound. What was once a tree—and then a snag, and then a rotting log—transforms yet again, becoming a nutrient-rich addition to the soil. This exchange of nutrients between the dead and the living is called nutrient cycling, and it is fundamental to the continuity of life on Earth.

# Trees and People

This story takes place in the Pacific Northwest, where forests and people have interacted since time immemorial. Long before nineteenth-century timber companies began logging Pacific Northwest forests, these lands were home to diverse Indigenous peoples who used forest resources sustainably. Native nations are still here today, and many are working to steward, restore, and diversify forests.

Forests are vital reservoirs of biodiversity. Because trees, logs, and forest soils store massive amounts of carbon, forests are also crucial to curbing climate change. We can all help protect forests. Learn more about conservation efforts happening in the Pacific Northwest and around the world at lesliebarnardbooth.com.

# Glossary

BACTERIA: Microscopic single-celled organisms, some of which are decomposers.

DECOMPOSERS: Organisms (mainly certain types of fungi and bacteria) that break down plant and animal remains, releasing nutrients that plants can absorb.

DECOMPOSITION: The process by which plant and animal remains are broken down into simpler forms.

ECOSYSTEM: An environment and all the living and nonliving things that interact within it.

FUNGI: Organisms including molds, yeasts, and mushrooms, some of which are decomposers.

HABITAT: A place where an organism naturally lives and grows.

INVERTEBRATES: Animals lacking a backbone, such as insects, worms, and mollusks.

NUTRIENT: A substance that an organism needs in order to live and grow.

NUTRIENT CYCLING: The process by which nutrients are continuously cycled through living and nonliving parts of an ecosystem.

ORGANISM: A living thing.

# Selected Sources

Arno, Stephen F., and Carl E. Fiedler. *Douglas Fir: The Story of the West's Most Remarkable Tree*. Seattle: Mountaineers Books, 2020.

Bull, Evelyn L. *The Value of Coarse Woody Debris to Vertebrates in the Pacific Northwest*. USDA Forest Service, 2002, www.fs.usda.gov/psw/publications/documents/psw_gtr181/016_Bull.pdf. PSW-GTR-181.

Marcot, Bruce G. *Ecosystem Processes Related to Wood Decay*. USDA Forest Service, 2017, www.fs.usda.gov/pnw/pubs/pnw_rn576.pdf. PNW-RN-576.

Montgomery, David R. *The Hidden Half of Nature: The Microbial Roots of Life and Health*. New York: W.W. Norton & Company, 2016.

Nelson, Melissa K., and Dan Shilling (eds). *Traditional Ecological Knowledge: Learning from Indigenous Practices for Environmental Sustainability*. Cambridge: Cambridge University Press, 2018.

Suzuki, David, and Wayne Grady. *Tree: A Life Story*. Vancouver: Greystone Books, 2018.

Wohlleben, Peter. *The Hidden Life of Trees*. London: William Collins, 2017.

Special thanks to wildlife biologist Lisa Bate, wildlife ecologist Barbara Garcia, plant scientist Soo-Hyung Kim and his lab, plant scientist Hannah Kinmonth-Schultz, and insect ecologist Timothy Schowalter for consulting on this book. Thanks as well to the following scientists, scholars, and educators for sharing their insights and expertise: Keith Aubry, Helen Davis, Eva Guggemos, Deidre Hayward, Cheyanne Heidt (Confederated Tribes of Grand Ronde), Mark Harmon, David G. Lewis (Confederated Tribes of Grand Ronde; Takelma, Chinook, Molalla, and Santiam Kalapuya), Bruce Marcot, Alexa Michel, Michael Paul Nelson, Catherine Raley, and Joshua L. Reid (Snohomish Indian Nation). It's been a joy and an honor to learn from all of you. Any errors are my own.